DIVINE RETRIBUTON

Comprehensive Prayers for Ancestral Retribution Redemption Recovery and Reconciliation

DRFAYE PASTOR-COACH

(c) DrFaye & Get Visible Studios All Rights Reserved 2024

Table of Contents

What Do You Wish To Accomplish By Activating This New Way Of Praying? 1

Preparing For The Journey 2

The Pathway To Miracles For African Americans 3

What You Will Experience 9

Introduction 12

The Birth Of Divine Retribution 17

The Impossibility Of Governmental Retribution 20

Universaal Prayer For Corporate Or Personal Prayers 24

Personal Version To Be Prayed Daily 28

Prayer To Be Prayed By Every African Living In Africa Today 33

Prayer For Black History Month Celebrating Our Legacy And Embracing Our Future 37

Prayer For Juneteenth Activation 42

Daily Prayers Of Activation 46

Monthly Prayers 50

Prayer For Black Teachers Returning To School 64

Holiday Prayers 69

Prayers For The 4 Seasons 76

Prayer Time Management 80

Acknowledgements 85

Hall Of Fame Dedication Page 90

Tribute Unrecognized African American Innovators 91

Prayers And Reflection For Three Innovators 97

WHAT DO YOU WISH TO ACCOMPLISH BY ACTIVATING THIS NEW WAY OF PRAYING?

What are the top 3 things you are praying for now?

- 1
- 2
- 3

After praying these prayers for at least 30 days, return to this list. Send me an email to coach@drfaye.com to let me share your testimony.

PREPARING FOR THE JOURNERY

1. **Create a Sacred Space**: Designate a quiet, comfortable space where you can read, pray, and reflect without interruptions. This will help you focus and fully engage with the material.

2. **Set Aside Dedicated Time**: Commit to a regular schedule for reading, praying, and journaling. Consistency is key to experiencing the full benefits of this journey.

3. **Open Your Heart and Mind**: Approach this book with an open heart and mind, ready to receive and act on divine guidance. Be prepared to confront and release past hurts, and embrace the promises of restoration and empowerment.

4. Engage Fully: Actively participate in the exercises, take detailed notes, and apply the activation steps. The more you engage, the more you will benefit from the transformative power of these prayers.

5. **Share the Journey**: Consider sharing this journey with trusted friends or family members. Discussing your experiences and insights can deepen your understanding and provide additional support.

THE PATHWAY TO MIRACLES FOR AFRICAN AMERICANS

"Divine Retribution" serves as a unique pathway to miracles for African Americans, this guide will emphasize the transformative power of the prayers and the specific journey toward reclaiming divine promises.

This step by step guide provides a comprehensive roadmap for you to fully engage with the prayers and teachings of "Divine Retribution," ensuring that you can unlock the miraculous power of God's promises in your lives. It emphasizes the importance of faith, action, community, and continuous growth, all grounded in a deep understanding of your divine heritage and identity as African Americans.

Step by Step Guide to Experiencing Miracles Through Divine Retribution

In this section, we delve into the unique power of "**Divine Retribution**" as a guide for African Americans to activate miracles in their lives. This book is more than a collection of prayers; it is a divine blueprint for reclaiming ancestral promises, embracing a new spiritual order, and experiencing the fullness of God's blessings. By following these steps, you can harness the power of the prayers and initiate a transformative journey not just for yourselves, but for generations to come.

Step 1: Foundation of Faith and Identity

Embrace Your Divine Heritage: Begin by acknowledging your identity as a beloved child of God and the rich heritage of your African ancestry. Recognize that your history is not just one of struggle, but also one of resilience, creativity, and divine purpose.

Daily Affirmation of Divine Retribution: Each day, declare that you are reclaiming everything that was lost or stolen from your ancestors. Affirm that you are worthy of receiving God's promises of restoration and abundance.

Scriptural Alignment: Engage with the scriptures provided in the book, allowing them to reinforce your faith and deepen your understanding of God's promises specifically for you as an African American.

Speak With Authority : Use the prayers in "Divine Retribution" with confidence and authority, knowing that your words are powerful and can effect change. Speak these prayers daily, covering every area of your life—spiritual, physical, mental, economic, social, and creative.

Personalization and Specificity: Tailor the prayers to your personal circumstances. Mention specific dreams, needs, and desires, believing that God is attentive to every detail of your life.

Visualize and Believe: As you pray, visualize the fulfillment of God's promises in your life. See yourself walking in abundance, health, and joy. Believe that these prayers are setting in motion the divine retribution owed to you and your lineage.

Step 3: Gratitude and Positive Expectation

Cultivate Gratitude: Start and end each day with gratitude. Thank God not only for what He has done but also for what He is about to do. Gratitude opens the door for more blessings and aligns your spirit with divine favor.

Expectation of Miracles: Live each day with an expectation of divine intervention and miracles. Actively look for signs of God's work in your life and celebrate every victory, big or small.

Faith Driven Actions: Take practical steps towards your goals, demonstrating your faith in action. Whether it's pursuing new opportunities, learning new skills, or nurturing relationships, act with the belief that God is guiding you.

Step 4: Community and Generational Impact

Engage in Collective Prayer: Join with others in your community to pray these prayers together. Collective prayer amplifies the power and impact, creating a strong spiritual force for change. Join our Wake Up and Pray with DrFaye Group on Facebook.

Share and Testify: Share the prayers and your experiences with others, encouraging them to embrace this journey. Your testimonies can inspire and empower others to seek God's retribution and blessings.

Mentor Futute Generations: Teach these prayers and principles to your children and encourage them to pass them on. Instill in them a strong sense of identity, purpose, and faith, ensuring that they continue to experience God's blessings.

Step 5: Continuous Learning and Spiritual Growth

Deepen Your Scriptural Knowledge: Continue to study the Bible and other spiritual texts that affirm God's promises of restoration and empowerment. Grow in your understanding of spiritual warfare, faith, and the power of prayer.

Participate in Spiritual Development: Attend workshops, seminars, and conferences that focus on spiritual growth and empowerment. Surround yourself with like minded individuals who support and uplift you.i.e https://christianwomenimpact.com

and https://kingdomwomenarerising.com

Reflect and Adapt: Regularly reflect on your spiritual journey and the results of your prayers. Adapt your approach as needed, staying aligned with God's leading and open to His guidance.

In Summary: A New Spiritual Order

Embrace the New Reality: Understand that "Divine Retribution" is not just a prayer book, but a catalyst for a new spiritual reality. As you practice these prayers, you are participating in the establishment of a new order where divine justice prevails, and God's blessings flow freely.

Commit to the Journey: Commit to reading these prayers 2-3 times daily, speaking life into your circumstances, and consistently expecting miracles. Remember, the more you engage with these prayers, the more you will experience the manifestations of God's promises.

Empower Others: Encourage others to join this movement of faith and restoration. Together, we can transform our communities and create a legacy of faith, prosperity, and empowerment for future generations.

Display 'Divine Retribution' prominently on your coffee table or another focal point. Growing up, I recall how my grandmother and mother always left the Family Bible open on the coffee table, ensuring everyone who passed by acknowledged its presence with respect. I encourage you to do the same with 'Divine Retribution.' This is why having both digital and hardcover versions is essential.

NOTES **DAY OF**

**DIVINE
RETRIBUTION**

WHAT YOU WILL EXPERIENCE

1. **Powerful Prayers for Transformation**: You will find prayers specifically crafted to address the spiritual, physical, mental, creative, and economic retribution owed to you and your ancestors. These prayers are designed to help you break generational curses, restore lost blessings, and activate miracles in your life.

2. **Personal Reflection and Journaling:** Throughout the book, you will encounter dedicated sections for personal reflection. These pages are meant for you to jot down your thoughts, insights, and revelations as you engage with the prayers and teachings. Use these spaces to capture your spiritual journey and track your growth.

3. **Goal Setting and Action Plans:** Setting goals is a crucial part of manifesting the promises and blessings outlined in this book. You will find prompts and templates to help you define your personal, spiritual, and financial goals. These sections will guide you in creating actionable plans to achieve these goals, ensuring that you actively participate in your transformation.

4. **Personal Mission for Prayer**: Developing a personal mission for prayer helps focus your spiritual intentions. You will be encouraged to articulate your mission, align it with the prayers in this book, and commit to regular prayer practices. This mission will serve as a guiding light for your journey, helping you stay focused and intentional.

5. Revelations and Spiritual Insights: As you pray and reflect, expect to receive divine revelations and spiritual insights. The book provides space for you to document these moments of clarity and inspiration. These insights will be invaluable as you move forward, offering guidance and encouragement.

6. **Weekly Activation Steps:** To help you integrate the teachings and prayers into your daily life, I suggest you conclude each week with practical activation steps. These steps should be designed to reinforce the lessons, encourage consistent practice, and help you experience tangible results.

Let the Journey Begin

INTRODUCTION

This book is dedicated to the ancestors who paved the way with their resilience, courage, and unwavering faith.

To all the brilliant African Americans, both living and departed, whose contributions have shaped history and enriched our world.

To every inventor, creator, author, and visionary whose genius was never acknowledged, your brilliance has not gone unnoticed. We honor your creativity and the legacies you left behind, knowing that your contributions continue to inspire and empower us.

To the mothers who bore children they never got to hold, and to the fathers who were separated from their children, we recognize your sacrifices and the profound pain of your loss. Your strength and love have been carried through the generations, nurturing a lineage of powerful, resilient souls.

To the countless individuals whose names and stories were erased or forgotten, we remember you. Your lives, your dreams, and your hopes are woven into the fabric of our identity and destiny. We stand on your shoulders, reclaiming the honor and recognition you deserved.

To the future generations, may you continue to honor our ancestors' legacy, walking in the strength and wisdom of those who came before us. May you experience the fullness of God's promises, and may your lives be a testament to the miracles and blessings that await us all.

This book is a testament to your enduring spirit and a commitment to ensuring that your contributions are never forgotten. It is a call to the living to rise, to remember, and to reclaim the fullness of the blessings and promises that are rightfully ours.

THE BIRTH OF DIVINE RETRIBUTION

In the beginning, when God created the heavens and the earth, He imbued humanity with dignity, purpose, and divine inheritance. Each soul, each lineage, carried within it the seed of God's glory, destined to flourish and multiply. For centuries, the African American community has borne the weight of profound injustices, their ancestors' dreams deferred, their rightful inheritances stolen. Yet, even amidst the trials, the divine promise remains: God restores, reconciles, redeems, and recovers all.

This book, titled "**Divine Retribution**," is a testament to that divine promise. It is a clarion call for every African American to rise and reclaim their God-given inheritance, a legacy that spans back to the beginning of time. Through powerful prayers, rooted in scripture and steeped in the wisdom of our ancestors, we seek to activate the promises of restoration and retribution that God has ordained for us.

The vision for "**Divine Retribution**" is clear: to empower the African American community with the spiritual tools necessary to reclaim their divine inheritance. It is a guide for daily prayer, a beacon of hope, and a manual for spiritual warfare. This book is not merely a collection of prayers; it is a movement, a transformative journey towards restoration and empowerment.

The importance of this book cannot be overstated. Every African American must read these prayers daily, for in doing so, they align themselves with God's promise of restoration. These prayers serve as a spiritual anchor, a daily reminder that no earthly power can thwart the plans and promises of the Almighty. Teaching these prayers to our children, and ensuring they pass them down to their children, creates a generational legacy of faith, resilience, and divine retribution.

The Power of Consistent Prayer

Just as the Bible exhorts us to speak the word of God consistently, this prayer must be read and declared 2-3 times a day. The Word of God promises that it will not return void but will accomplish that which we please and prosper in the thing where it is sent (Isaiah 55:11). By committing to this practice, you will experience a profound transformation in your life. The more you pray, the stronger the manifestations of God's promises will become. This disciplined practice will embed the divine truths deep within your spirit, mind, and soul, empowering you to live out your God-given destiny.

NOTES   **DAY OF**

DIVINE RETRIBUTION

THE IMPOSSIBILITY OF GOVERNMENTAL RETRIBUTION

It is crucial to understand that retribution from earthly governments is an impossibility. While justice may be sought and reparations demanded, true restoration can only come from the divine hand of God. The presence and power of God have promised to restore the years that the cankerworm, the locust, and the caterpillar have stolen (Joel 2:25).

This promise is eternal, unwavering, and personalized for the African American community.

Scriptural Foundation The foundation of "Divine Retribution" is deeply rooted in scripture. Throughout the Bible, we find God's unwavering commitment to restore, reconcile, redeem, and recover all that was lost. These scriptures, while universal, hold a profound personal significance for African Americans. They speak directly to the heart of our struggles and the promise of our deliverance.

1. Restoration: "I will restore to you the years that the swarming locust has eaten..." (Joel 2:25). This promise of restoration is a divine assurance that every loss, every stolen dream, will be restored manifold.

2. Reconciliation: "All this is from God, who reconciled us to himself through Christ and gave us the ministry of reconciliation" (2 Corinthians 5:18). Through Christ, we are reconciled to God and to one another, healing the wounds of division and oppression.

3. Redemption: "In him, we have redemption through his blood, the forgiveness of sins, in accordance with the riches of God's grace" (Ephesians 1:7). Our redemption is a testament to God's grace, lifting us from the depths of sin and restoring us to our rightful place.

4. Recovery: "And I will restore your fortunes and gather you from all the nations and all the places where I have driven you, declares the Lord, and I will bring you back to the place from which I sent you into exile" (Jeremiah 29:14). God's promise to recover and restore our fortunes speaks directly to the African American experience, promising a return to glory and prosperity.

Personalizing the Promise While these scriptures are for everyone, "Divine Retribution" seeks to personalize these promises for African Americans. Our history is unique, marked by extraordinary trials and triumphs. The scriptures, therefore, hold a unique resonance for us, speaking to our collective journey and individual lives.

Each prayer in this book is crafted to invoke these divine promises, calling forth restoration, reconciliation, redemption, and recovery. As you read and pray, envision the generational curses breaking, the stolen wealth returning, and the divine inheritance manifesting in your life and the lives of your descendants.

"Divine Retribution" is more than a book; it is a movement towards divine justice and spiritual empowerment. By embracing these prayers and teachings, we align ourselves with God's eternal promise to restore all that was lost. Let us commit to praying these prayers daily, teaching them to our children, and passing them down through the generations.

In doing so, we affirm our faith in God's unwavering promise and take a bold step towards reclaiming our divine inheritance. The journey of restoration begins now, and through the power of prayer, we will see the fulfillment of God's promises in our lives and our community.

Let us read and declare these prayers 2-3 times a day, embedding the divine truths deep within our spirits. As we commit to this practice, we will experience the manifestations of God's promises with increasing strength and clarity. The power of God's word, spoken consistently, will transform our lives and the lives of future generations. Together, let us reclaim our divine inheritance and walk boldly into the destiny that God has ordained for us.

NOTES   DAY OF

DIVINE
RETRIBUTION

UNIVERSAAL PRAYER FOR CORPORATE OR PERSONAL PRAYERS

Beloved brothers and sisters, today we gather in unity and strength to invoke the divine power bestowed upon us by our Creator. We stand on behalf of our ancestors, whose lives, dreams, and legacies were unjustly stolen. As we lift our voices in this powerful prayer, let us remember that we are part of something greater. We are the living legacy of those who came before us, and through this prayer, we call forth the Ancestral Retribution Redemption Recovery and Reconciliation, that is rightfully ours. Let us prepare our hearts and minds to receive and activate this divine inheritance.

Our Father Who Lives Within Us,

We come before You today, united in spirit, purpose, and determination, invoking the divine authority and inheritance that is ours as Your children. We stand on behalf of our African ancestors, whose wealth, dignity, and lives were unjustly stolen and erased from history. This prayer reaches back to the beginning of time, reclaiming and restoring all that was taken.

Lord, we acknowledge the profound physical, mental, and spiritual injustices inflicted upon our forebears. We recognize the gold, diamonds, pearls, rubies, and treasures that were stolen from Africa, and the broken promises of those who exploited and enslaved our people. Today, we call forth those promises and treasures, not just for ourselves, but for our entire lineage.

Physical Restoration

In the mighty name of Jesus, we declare that no system of this world can limit the divine inheritance bestowed upon us. We activate this prayer without bounds, calling into our present reality the full manifestation of every promise made to our ancestors. We summon forth every treasure, every ounce of wealth, and every unfulfilled dream that belongs to our bloodline.

We call forth the physical restoration of our ancestors' toil. Every drop of sweat, every ounce of strength, every piece of land, and every home that was taken. We claim physical retribution for the bodies that were broken, the lives that were cut short, and the generations that were physically oppressed.

Mental Restoration

We speak mental restoration and liberation over our lineage. For the minds that were shackled, the dreams that were deferred, and the intellectual potentials that were suppressed. We declare that the mental chains of oppression are broken. We reclaim the wisdom, creativity, and brilliance that was inherent in our ancestors and call it forth into our lives now.

Creative Restoration

We call forth the restoration of ideas, inventions, creativity, and patents that were stolen and credited to others. We reclaim the intellectual property, the innovative spirit, and the creative genius of our ancestors. We declare that these gifts are reactivated within us, bringing forth new innovations, creations, and breakthroughs in our time.

Spiritual Restoration

We call forth spiritual restoration for the souls that were wounded and the faith that was tested. We declare that the spiritual strength and resilience of our ancestors are activated within us. We summon the divine connection, the unwavering faith, and the spiritual inheritance that belongs to us.

Economic Restoration

We call forth the economic retribution for the wealth that was stolen. We summon the gold, the diamonds, the lands, and the resources that were taken. We declare that the economic prosperity of our ancestors is restored to us, with interest. We activate the wealth within our DNA, calling it forth into our present reality.

Social Restoration

We speak social retribution and restoration over our lineage. For the communities that were torn apart, the families that were separated, and the cultures that were suppressed. We declare that the social fabric of our heritage is mended. We call forth unity, strength, and solidarity within our communities.

In the name of Jesus, we decree that this wealth, retribution, and restoration are being activated within us. We speak life into the dreams of our ancestors, calling them forth to be realized in our time. We declare that the power of their legacy will not be erased but will shine brightly through us.

Lord, we thank You for hearing our prayer. We receive this retribution and restoration with open hearts, knowing that we are part of something far greater than ourselves. We stand as the living legacy of our ancestors, declaring that their dreams, their wealth, and their dignity are restored in us.

In Conclusion

As we conclude this powerful prayer, let us hold fast to the truth that we are the living testament of our ancestors' dreams and sacrifices. Their strength flows through our veins, and their hopes are alive in our hearts. With every step we take, we carry their legacy forward. Let us walk in the fullness of our restored inheritance, with heads held high and spirits unbroken. Together, we stand, reclaiming our rightful place in history and forging a future filled with promise and divine inheritance. So Be it!

NOTES DAY OF

DIVINE
RETRIBUTION

PERSONAL VERSION TO BE PRAYED DAILY

My Father Who Lives Within Me

I come before You today, in spirit, purpose, and determination, invoking the divine authority and inheritance that is mine as Your child. I stand on behalf of my African ancestors, whose wealth, dignity, and lives were unjustly stolen and erased from history. This prayer reaches back to the beginning of time, reclaiming and restoring all that was taken.

Lord, I acknowledge the profound physical, mental, and spiritual injustices inflicted upon my forebears. I recognize the gold, diamonds, pearls, rubies, and treasures that were stolen from Africa, and the broken promises of those who exploited and enslaved my people. Today, I call forth those promises and treasures, not just for myself, but for my entire lineage.

Physical Restoration

In the mighty name of Jesus, I declare that no system of this world can limit the divine inheritance bestowed upon me. I activate this prayer without bounds, calling into my present reality the full manifestation of every promise made to my ancestors. I summon forth every treasure, every ounce of wealth, and every unfulfilled dream that belongs to my bloodline.

I call forth the physical restoration of my ancestors' toil. Every drop of sweat, every ounce of strength, every piece of land, and every home that was taken. I claim physical retribution for the bodies that were broken, the lives that were cut short, and the generations that were physically oppressed. Lord, I pray for the healing of generational wounds, the restoration of physical health, and the rebuilding of my body's strength. I declare that every cell, every bone, and every organ in my body is renewed and restored to its original divine design.

Mental Restoration

I speak mental restoration and liberation over my lineage. For the minds that were shackled, the dreams that were deferred, and the intellectual potentials that were suppressed. I declare that the mental chains of oppression are broken. I reclaim the wisdom, creativity, and brilliance that was inherent in my ancestors and call it forth into my life now. I pray for the renewal of my mind, for clarity of thought, and for the courage to dream boldly. Let every mental barrier and every lie of inferiority be cast down. I declare that my mind is free, sharp, and aligned with divine wisdom.

Creative Restoration

I call forth the restoration of ideas, inventions, creativity, and patents that were stolen and credited to others. I reclaim the intellectual property, the innovative spirit, and the creative genius of my ancestors. I declare that these gifts are reactivated within me, bringing forth new innovations, creations, and breakthroughs in my time. Lord, I ask for the outpouring of Your creative spirit upon me. Let me birth new ideas, inventions, and artistic expressions that will transform my community and the world. I declare that every creative blockage is removed and that I am flowing in divine creativity and innovation.

Spiritual Restoration

I call forth spiritual restoration for the souls that were wounded and the faith that was tested. I declare that the spiritual strength and resilience of my ancestors are activated within me. I summon the divine connection, the unwavering faith, and the spiritual inheritance that belongs to me. Father, I pray for a deepening of my relationship with You. Let my spirit be renewed and my faith be fortified. I ask for a fresh outpouring of Your

Holy Spirit to guide, comfort, and empower me. I declare that my spiritual heritage is restored and that I walk in divine purpose and calling.

Economic Restoration

I call forth the economic retribution for the wealth that was stolen. I summon the gold, the diamonds, the lands, and the resources that were taken. I declare that the economic prosperity of my ancestors is restored to me, with interest. I activate the wealth within my DNA, calling it forth into my present reality. Lord, I pray for financial breakthroughs, for the release of resources, and for the wisdom to steward them well. Let me build generational wealth and create economic opportunities for my community. I declare that poverty is broken and that abundance is my portion.

Social Restoration

I speak social retribution and restoration over my lineage. For the communities that were torn apart, the families that were separated, and the cultures that were suppressed. I declare that the social fabric of my heritage is mended. I call forth unity, strength, and solidarity within my community. Father, I pray for the restoration of relationships, for the healing of broken families, and for the revival of my cultural heritage. Let me build strong, vibrant communities where love, respect, and unity prevail. I declare that our social structures are restored and that we thrive together in harmony.

In the name of Jesus, I decree that this wealth, retribution, and restoration are being activated within me. I speak life into the dreams of my ancestors, calling them forth to be realized in my time. I declare that the power of their legacy will not be erased but will shine brightly through me.

Lord, I thank You for hearing my prayer. I receive this retribution and restoration with an open heart, knowing that I am part of something far greater than myself. I stand as the living legacy of my ancestors, declaring that their dreams, their wealth, and their dignity are restored in me.

In Conclusion

As I conclude this powerful prayer, I hold fast to the truth that I am the living testament of my ancestors' dreams and sacrifices. Their strength flows through my veins, and their hopes are alive in my heart. With every step I take, I carry their legacy forward. Let me walk in the fullness of my restored inheritance, with my head held high and spirit unbroken. Together, we stand, reclaiming our rightful place in history and forging a future filled with promise and divine abundance. And so it is!

NOTES **DAY OF**

DIVINE
RETRIBUTION

PRAYER TO BE PRAYED BY EVERY AFRICAN LIVING IN AFRICA TODAY

Beloved brothers and sisters, we gather in unity and strength to invoke the divine power bestowed upon us by our Creator. Today, we lift our voices not only for those who have been dispersed across the globe but also for our brothers and sisters who remain in the motherland of Africa. This prayer seeks to honor our roots and reclaim the divine inheritance and blessings intended for the native people of Africa. Let us open our hearts to receive and activate this powerful prayer.

Our Father Who Lives Within Us,

We come before You today, united in spirit and purpose, invoking the divine authority and inheritance that is ours as Your children. We stand on behalf of our African ancestors and our brothers and sisters who remain in Africa, honoring our roots and reclaiming the blessings and prosperity that are rightfully ours.

Lord, we acknowledge the profound historical, economic, social, and spiritual challenges faced by the native people of Africa. We recognize the wealth, resources, and potentials that have been unjustly exploited. Today, we call forth the restoration and empowerment of the native African people, reclaiming their divine inheritance.

Physical Restoration

In the mighty name of Jesus, we declare that no system of this world can limit the divine inheritance bestowed upon the people of Africa. We activate this prayer without bounds, calling into present reality the full manifestation of every promise made to our ancestors. We summon forth every treasure, every ounce of wealth, and every unfulfilled dream that belongs to the African people.

We call forth the physical restoration of the land and its people. Every piece of land, every home, every resource that was taken. We claim physical retribution for the bodies that were broken, the lives that were cut short, and the generations that were physically oppressed. Lord, we pray for the healing of generational wounds, the restoration of physical health, and the rebuilding of the bodies' strength. We declare that every cell, every bone, and every organ in the bodies of African people is renewed and restored to its original divine design.

Mental Restoration

We speak mental restoration and liberation over the native African people. For the minds that were shackled, the dreams that were deferred, and the intellectual potentials that were suppressed. We declare that the mental chains of oppression are broken. We reclaim the wisdom, creativity, and brilliance that are inherent in the African people and call it forth into their lives now. We pray for the renewal of minds, for clarity of thought, and for the courage to dream boldly. Let every mental barrier and every lie of inferiority be cast down. We declare that the minds of African people are free, sharp, and aligned with divine wisdom.

Creative Restoration

We call forth the restoration of ideas, inventions, creativity, and patents that were stolen and credited to others. We reclaim the intellectual property, the innovative spirit, and the creative genius of the African people. We declare that these gifts are reactivated within them, bringing forth new innovations, creations, and breakthroughs in their time. Lord, we ask for the outpouring of Your creative spirit upon the native African people. Let them birth new ideas, inventions, and artistic expressions that will transform their communities and the world. We declare that every creative blockage is removed and that they are flowing in divine creativity and innovation.

Spiritual Restoration

We call forth spiritual restoration for the souls that were wounded and the faith that was tested. We declare that the spiritual strength and resilience of the African people are activated within them. We summon the divine connection, the unwavering faith, and the spiritual inheritance that belongs to them. Father, we pray for a deepening of their relationship with You. Let their spirits be renewed and their faith be fortified. We ask for a fresh outpouring of Your Holy Spirit to guide, comfort, and empower them. We declare that their spiritual heritage is restored and that they walk in divine purpose and calling.

Economic Restoration

We call forth the economic retribution for the wealth that was stolen. We summon the gold, the diamonds, the lands, and the resources that were taken. We declare that the economic prosperity of the African people is restored to them, with interest. We activate the wealth within their DNA, calling it forth into their present reality. Lord, we pray for financial breakthroughs, for the release of resources, and for the wisdom to steward them well. Let them build generational wealth and create economic opportunities for their communities. We declare that poverty is broken and that abundance is their portion.

Social Restoration

We speak social retribution and restoration over the native African people. For the communities that were torn apart, the families that were separated, and the cultures that were suppressed. We declare that the social fabric of their heritage is mended. We call forth unity, strength, and solidarity within their communities.

NOTES DAY OF

DIVINE
RETRIBUTION

PRAYER FOR BLACK HISTORY MONTH CELEBRATING OUR LEGACY AND EMBRACING OUR FUTURE

This is a comprehensive prayer for Black History Month, designed to celebrate, honor, and inspire African Americans for generations to come. This prayer is a powerful addition, emphasizing the significance of Black History Month and the enduring legacy of African Americans.

PRAYER

Father Who Lives Within Me, As we gather to honor Black History Month, we come before You with hearts full of gratitude, reverence, and hope. We celebrate the rich heritage and extraordinary contributions of African Americans throughout history. We acknowledge the trials and triumphs, the struggles and successes, and the enduring spirit of our ancestors who paved the way for us.

Celebration of Heritage

Lord, we thank You for the rich cultural heritage and the profound legacy of African Americans. We celebrate the artists, scholars, activists, and leaders who have made significant contributions to every facet of society. We honor their courage, creativity, and unwavering determination. As it is written in Psalm 78:4, "We will not hide them from their descendants; we will tell the next generation the praiseworthy deeds of the Lord, His power, and the wonders He has done."

Acknowledgment of Struggles

Father, we remember the suffering and oppression endured by our ancestors. We acknowledge the pain of slavery, segregation, and systemic racism that sought to devalue and dehumanize. Yet, through it all, You have been our refuge and strength. As we reflect on our history, we also recognize Your faithfulness and Your promise in Isaiah 40:31: "But those who hope in the Lord will renew their strength. They will soar on wings like eagles; they will run and not grow weary, they will walk and not be faint."

Empowerment for the Present

Lord, empower us today as we continue to fight for justice, equality, and freedom. Fill us with Your wisdom and courage to stand against injustice and to advocate for righteousness. Guide our leaders, communities, and families as we work together to build a brighter future. Remind us of Your words in Micah 6:8, "He has shown you, O mortal, what is good. And what does the Lord require of you? To act justly and to love mercy and to walk humbly with your God."

Inspiration for the Future

We pray for the next generation, that they may be inspired by the legacy of those who came before them. Let them know their worth and potential in You. Equip them with the knowledge and strength to pursue their dreams and to make meaningful contributions to the world. As it says in Jeremiah 29:11, "For I know the plans I have for you, declares the Lord, plans to prosper you and not to harm you, plans to give you hope and a future."

Acknowledging Contributions

Father, we recognize and celebrate the contributions of African Americans in every field

—science, art, literature, politics, sports, and beyond. We thank You for the brilliance, creativity, and resilience that have shaped and continue to shape our world. May their achievements be a testament to Your glory and a source of inspiration for all. Remind us of Your promise in Ephesians 2:10, "For we are God's handiwork, created in Christ Jesus to do good works, which God prepared in advance for us to do."

Restoration and Healing

We pray for the healing of generational wounds and the restoration of brokenness within our communities. Restore the years that have been lost, the opportunities that were denied, and the dreams that were deferred. As You promised in Joel 2:25, "I will restore to you the years that the locust hath eaten." Heal our hearts, minds, and spirits, and unite us in love and purpose.

Unity and Strength

Lord, let this month be a time of unity, reflection, and celebration. Strengthen our bonds as a community and help us to support and uplift one another. Let the spirit of unity and love prevail among us, as we work together to create a world where justice and equality are realized. As it is written in Psalm 133:1, "How good and pleasant it is when God's people live together in unity!"

Spiritual Growth

We pray for spiritual growth and a deeper connection with You. Help us to seek Your guidance and wisdom in all that we do. Let our faith be a source of strength and hope as we navigate the challenges and opportunities before us. Remind us of Your promise in Philippians 4:13, "I can do all this through Him who gives me strength."

Commitment to Legacy

Finally, Lord, we commit ourselves to preserving and honoring the legacy of African Americans. Let us teach our children and their children about the sacrifices, achievements, and contributions of their ancestors. May they grow up with a strong sense of identity, purpose, and pride. Empower us to continue the work of our forebears and to build a future that reflects Your justice, mercy, and love.

DIVINE RETRIBUTON

We thank You, Lord, for Your faithfulness, Your love, and Your grace. We trust in Your promises and believe that You are working all things together for our good. We commit ourselves to Your hands, knowing that You are able to do exceedingly abundantly above all that we ask or think, according to the power that works in us (Ephesians 3:20).

In the name of Jesus, who came to set the captives free, we declare restoration, healing, and empowerment over every life touched by the legacy of Black History Month. Amen.

This prayer serves as a powerful reminder of the rich heritage, enduring strength, and divine purpose of African Americans, inspiring us to honor the past, embrace the present, and look forward to a future filled with hope and promise.

NOTES DAY OF

DIVINE
RETRIBUTION

PRAYER FOR JUNETEENTH ACTIVATION

Prayer for Juneteenth: Restoration and Empowerment

Our Father, We come before You on this significant and sacred day of Juneteenth, a day that marks the end of slavery and the beginning of a journey toward freedom and justice for African Americans. We acknowledge the pain and heartache that our ancestors endured, the suffering they faced, and the resilience they demonstrated.

Today, we honor their legacy and the strength that has carried us through the generations.

Lord, Your Word assures us that You are a God of restoration. In Joel 2:25, You promise, "I will restore to you the years that the locust hath eaten, the cankerworm, and the caterpillar, and the palmerworm, my great army which I sent among you." We stand on this promise today, believing that You will restore all that has been lost to those who have been most vulnerable.

Father, we ask for the restoration of our communities, the rebuilding of broken homes, and the healing of wounded hearts. We pray for the restoration of hope to those who have felt hopeless, the restoration of joy to those who have experienced sorrow, and the restoration of wealth and opportunities to those who have been unjustly deprived. As it is written in Isaiah 61:7, "Instead of your shame you will receive a double portion, and instead of disgrace you will rejoice in your inheritance. And so you will inherit a double portion in your land, and everlasting joy will be yours."

Lord, we declare Your word in Jeremiah 30:17 over our lives: "For I will restore health unto thee, and I will heal thee of thy wounds, saith the Lord; because they called thee an Outcast, saying, This is Zion, whom no man seeketh after." We ask for healing for every wound inflicted by generations of injustice, for every scar left by racism, discrimination, and inequality. Heal our minds, our bodies, and our spirits, O Lord.

Empower us, O Lord, with the courage and confidence to step into the fullness of the destiny You have for us. Let the spirit of unity, love, and forgiveness prevail among us, as we strive to uplift and support one another in our communities. As we pursue justice and equity, remind us of Your words in Micah 6:8: "He has shown you, O mortal, what is good. And what does the Lord require of you? To act justly and to love mercy and to walk humbly with your God."

We pray for the dismantling of systemic racism and the eradication of all forms of injustice. Guide our leaders, give them wisdom, and fill them with compassion and a genuine desire for equality. We declare Your promise in Isaiah 42:16, "I will lead the blind by ways they have not known, along unfamiliar paths I will guide them; I will turn the darkness into light before them and make the rough places smooth. These are the things I will do; I will not forsake them."

Lord, we lift up the African American women professionals and leaders, who are striving to make a lasting impact in the world. Grant them the strength and vision to lead with integrity, wisdom, and grace. Empower them to break barriers, shatter glass ceilings, and create pathways for future generations. Let their success be a testament to Your glory and a beacon of hope for others.

As we remember the emancipation and the ongoing struggle for true freedom, fill our hearts with Your peace, which surpasses all understanding, and guide our steps with Your wisdom. Let Your Holy Spirit ignite within us a renewed sense of purpose, as we work towards closing the wealth gap and achieving lasting impact. We declare Your promise in Deuteronomy 30:3-5, "Then the Lord your God will restore your fortunes and have compassion on you and gather you again from all the nations where He scattered you. Even if you have been banished to the most distant land under the heavens, from there the Lord your God will gather you and bring you back. He will bring you to the land that belonged to your ancestors, and you will take possession of it. He will make you more prosperous and numerous than your ancestors."

We thank You, Lord, for Your faithfulness, Your love, and Your mercy. We trust in Your promises and believe that You are working all things together for our good. We commit ourselves to Your hands, knowing that You are able to do exceedingly abundantly above all that we ask or think, according to the power that works in us (Ephesians 3:20).

In the name of Jesus, who came to set the captives free, we declare restoration, healing, and empowerment over every life touched by the legacy of Juneteenth. **Amen.**

NOTES   **DAY OF**

DIVINE RETRIBUTION

DAILY PRAYERS OF ACTIVATION

Creating daily prayers of activation for each day of the week, aligned with the themes of restoration and retribution, is a powerful way to keep your focus and momentum.

Each day we address specific aspects of restoration, ensuring a comprehensive approach over the week. Here's a structure for each day of the week.

Sunday: Spiritual Restoration

Good Morning, Sunday! Today, I call forth the spiritual promises and blessings destined for my ancestors. I activate the divine connection, unwavering faith, and spiritual inheritance that are mine. Heavenly Father, as I stand on behalf of my ancestors, I reclaim the spiritual strength and resilience that were suppressed. Let my spirit be renewed and my faith be fortified. I pray for a fresh outpouring of Your Holy Spirit to guide, comfort, and empower me. Today, I walk in divine purpose and calling. **Amen.**

Monday: Physical Restoration

Good Morning, Monday! I call you forth to bring physical restoration and health, honoring the bodies of my ancestors who endured immense suffering. I declare healing over every cell, every bone, and every organ in my body. Father, restore the physical vitality that was stolen, heal generational wounds, and rebuild our physical strength. I claim the physical inheritance of health, longevity, and strength that was meant for my ancestors. Today, I receive physical wholeness and vitality in abundance. **Amen.**

Tuesday: Mental Restoration

Good Morning, Tuesday! Today, I call forth the mental restoration and liberation promised to my ancestors. I declare clarity of thought, wisdom, and the courage to dream boldly. I break every mental barrier and lie of inferiority. Father, renew my mind and release the brilliance, creativity, and intellectual prowess that were suppressed in my lineage. Let my mind be sharp, free, and aligned with divine wisdom. I embrace the mental inheritance of strength, creativity, and wisdom today. **Amen.**

Wednesday: Creative Restoration

Good Morning, Wednesday! I call you forth to bring creative restoration and innovation. I reclaim the ideas, inventions, creativity, and patents stolen from my ancestors. Father, pour out Your creative spirit upon me, igniting new ideas, inventions, and artistic expressions. Let my creativity flow freely and let it transform my life and community. I receive the creative inheritance of innovation and artistic brilliance that is rightfully mine. Today, I walk in divine creativity and innovation. **Amen.**

Thursday: Economic Restoration

Good Morning, Thursday! I call you forth to bring economic restoration and abundance. I summon the wealth, resources, and prosperity that were stolen from my ancestors.

Father, restore the gold, the diamonds, the lands, and the economic opportunities that were taken. I declare financial breakthroughs and wisdom to steward resources well. Let my economic prosperity be restored with interest. Today, I activate the wealth within my DNA and claim abundance and financial freedom. **Amen.**

Friday: Social Restoration

Good Morning, Friday! I call you forth to bring social restoration and unity. I reclaim the communities, families, and cultures that were torn apart and suppressed. Father, mend the social fabric of our heritage. I declare unity, strength, and solidarity within my community. Let the social legacy of my ancestors be restored and let us build strong, supportive, and thriving communities. Today, I walk in social harmony and collective strength. Amen.

Saturday: Legacy Restoration

Good Morning, Saturday! I call you forth to bring legacy restoration and fulfillment. I activate the dreams, visions, and aspirations of my ancestors that were never realized. Father, let their unfulfilled promises and dreams come to fruition in my lifetime. I declare that the generational curses are broken, and the divine inheritance of my ancestors is manifesting in me. Let the legacy of my ancestors be honored and fulfilled through my life and the lives of my descendants. Today, I embrace and activate my divine legacy. **Amen**

By following this structure, each day focuses on a specific aspect of restoration and retribution, allowing for a holistic and continuous spiritual practice. This repetition and daily focus will help embed the divine promises deeply within the spirit and life of every individual who prays these prayers.

NOTES   DAY OF

DIVINE
RETRIBUTION

MONTHLY PRAYERS

January: New Beginnings and Resolutions Purpose:

January represents a time of new beginnings and setting resolutions. Monthly prayers in January focus on starting the year with a clean slate, aligning oneself with God's vision, and setting intentions for personal and spiritual growth.

Why: Praying at the start of the year helps to set a positive tone and spiritual direction for the months ahead. It encourages reflection on past achievements and lessons, while inviting divine guidance for the year to come.

January Historical Reflection

In January 1966, the first Kwanzaa was celebrated, honoring African heritage and culture. In January 1865, Congress passed the 13th Amendment, abolishing slavery in the United States.

Quote/Scripture: "Behold, I will do a new thing; now it shall spring forth; shall ye not know it? I will even make a way in the wilderness and rivers in the desert." (Isaiah 43:19)

Prayer: As we enter the new year, we reflect on the passage of the 13th Amendment and the end of slavery. Let this month be a time of new beginnings and fresh starts. Renew our spirits, and guide us in Your ways. Help us to remember the sacrifices of our ancestors and to honor their legacy by striving for justice and equality Lord, as we begin this new year, renew our strength and vision. May January be a month of fresh starts and divine opportunities. Guide us in Your wisdom and light our path. **Amen.**

February: Heritage and Identity Purpose:

February, recognized as Black History Month, is dedicated to celebrating African American heritage and contributions. The prayers focus on embracing and honoring one's identity and acknowledging the legacy of ancestors.

Why: Praying during this month reinforces the value of heritage and instills pride in one's identity. It helps to connect with the historical significance and continue the legacy of resilience and achievement.

February Historical Reflection:

February is Black History Month, established to honor the achievements and contributions of African Americans throughout history.

Quote/Scripture: "The Lord is my light and my salvation; whom shall I fear? The Lord is the strength of my life; of whom shall I be afraid?" (Psalm 27:1)

Prayer: Father, During Black History Month, we celebrate the rich heritage and contributions of African Americans. We thank You for the resilience, strength, and achievements of our ancestors. Let this month be a time of reflection, learning, and growth. Empower us to continue their legacy and to make a positive impact in our communities. during this Black History Month, we honor the legacy of our ancestors. Let their stories inspire us to strive for excellence and justice in all we do. Bless us with courage and unity. **Amen.**

March: Renewal and Growth Purpose:

March often symbolizes the beginning of spring and renewal. Prayers in March are aimed at spiritual renewal, personal growth, and transformation.

Why: As nature begins to renew itself, this is a perfect time to seek spiritual rejuvenation and growth. It allows individuals to realign their goals and aspirations with divine purpose.

March Historical Reflection:

In March 1965, the Selma to Montgomery marches took place, pivotal events in the Civil Rights Movement.

Quote/Scripture: "But let justice roll on like a river, righteousness like a never-failing stream!" (Amos 5:24)

Prayer: Heavenly Father, As we remember the Selma to Montgomery marches, we pray for justice and equality in our society. Strengthen our resolve to fight for the rights of all people. Let this month be a time of action and advocacy. Guide us in our efforts to bring about positive change and to honor the legacy of those who fought for our freedoms, let March be a time of renewal and growth. Help us to shed the old and embrace the new, trusting in Your plan for our lives. **Amen.**

April: Overcoming Challenges Purpose:

April is a time of reflection on overcoming personal and collective challenges. Prayers in this month focus on resilience, strength, and perseverance.

Why: Praying for strength during difficult times fosters hope and courage. It provides support and encouragement to overcome obstacles and challenges.

April Historical Reflection:

On April 4, 1968, Dr. Martin Luther King Jr. was assassinated, a turning point in the struggle for civil rights.

Quote/Scripture: "Blessed are those who mourn, for they will be comforted." (Matthew 5:4)

Prayer: As we reflect on the life and legacy of Dr. Martin Luther King Jr., we mourn his loss and the loss of so many who fought for justice. Comfort us in our grief and strengthen our resolve to continue their work. Let this month be a time of remembrance and dedication to the principles of equality and justice.,in this month of new beginnings, we celebrate the resurrection of Your Son. Fill our hearts with hope and joy as we walk in the light of Your love and promises. **Amen.**

May: Gratitude and Reflection Purpose:

May is often associated with gratitude and reflection. Prayers this month focus on thanking God for blessings, acknowledging growth, and reflecting on the journey.

Prayer: Gratitude opens the heart to receive more blessings. Reflecting on progress helps to appreciate and acknowledge divine provision and guidance.

DIVINE RETRIBUTON

May Historical Reflection:

In May 1954, the Supreme Court ruled in Brown v. Board of Education that racial segregation in public schools was unconstitutional. In May 1963, the Birmingham Children's Crusade brought national attention to the civil rights movement and the fight against segregation.

Quote/Scripture: "Train up a child in the way he should go, and when he is old, he will not depart from it." (Proverbs 22:6)

"Let the little children come to me, and do not hinder them, for the kingdom of heaven belongs to such as these." (Matthew 19:14)

Prayer: Gracious God, as we honor mothers and maternal figures this month, we thank You for their nurturing and strength. We remember the bravery of the children who marched in Birmingham and the impact of their actions. Let this month be a time of courage and determination in the fight for justice. Guide us in our efforts to create a better world for future generations. Bless all women who give life and love to others. **Amen**

June: Celebration and Empowerment Purpose:

June marks celebrations like Juneteenth and other significant events. Prayers in June focus on empowerment, celebration of achievements, and envisioning a brighter future. Although, I have included a separate prayer for Juneteenth, I felt it necessary to add one here as well.

Why: Celebrating achievements and empowering oneself reinforces the strength and resilience of African American history. It encourages continued progress and success.

June Historical Reflection:

One of the most historically significant events for the African American community that occurred in June is the celebration of Juneteenth.

Juneteenth, celebrated on June 19th, commemorates the announcement of the abolition of slavery in Texas in 1865, and more generally the emancipation of enslaved African Americans throughout the Confederate South.

Historical Significance of Juneteenth

1. End of Slavery in Texas: Event: On June 19, 1865, Union General Gordon Granger arrived in Galveston, Texas, and announced General Order No. 3, which declared that all enslaved people in Texas were free. This announcement came more than two years after President Abraham Lincoln had issued the Emancipation Proclamation on January 1, 1863.

Significance: This day is significant as it symbolizes the end of slavery in the United States, marking the last group of enslaved African Americans to be informed of their freedom.

2. Celebration of Freedom: Traditions: Juneteenth is celebrated with community gatherings, historical reenactments, educational events, and cultural festivities that highlight African American heritage and achievements.

3. Recognition and Reflection: Legacy: Juneteenth serves as a time to reflect on the struggles and contributions of African Americans throughout history and to recognize the ongoing fight for equality and justice.

Prayer for Juneteenth Heavenly Father, We come before You on this historic and joyous day of Juneteenth, a day that marks the end of slavery and the beginning of true freedom for African Americans. We thank You for the resilience and strength of our ancestors who endured unimaginable hardships and for the progress that has been made since that day in 1865. Lord, as we celebrate Juneteenth, we remember the struggles and sacrifices of those who came before us.

We honor their legacy and the fight for justice and equality that continues to this day. We ask for Your guidance and strength as we work towards a more just and equitable society. Help us to live in the spirit of freedom and to extend that freedom to all our brothers and sisters. Fill our hearts with love, compassion, and understanding, and let us be instruments of Your peace and justice in the world.

We pray for the healing of our communities, the restoration of our families, and the empowerment of every individual to reach their God given potential. May the spirit of Juneteenth inspire us to continue the fight for equality and to build a future where everyone is free to live, work, and thrive. In the name of Jesus, who came to set the captives free, we pray. **Amen.**

Quote/Scripture: "So if the Son sets you free, you will be free indeed." (John 8:36)

References for Juneteenth: "On Juneteenth" by Annette GordonReed "Juneteenth: A Celebration of Freedom" by Charles A. Taylor National Museum of African American History & Culture Smithsonian Institution

July: Freedom and Independence Purpose:

July is associated with themes of freedom and independence. Prayers this month focus on embracing freedom, independence, and the pursuit of personal and spiritual goals. That being said, I would be remiss in not sharing the historical facts as they relate to July 4th and African Americans:

African Americans may observe July 4th differently due to its complex historical implications.

Here are several reasons why some African Americans may approach July 4th with ambivalence or caution:

Historical Context

1. Lack of Freedom for Enslaved People: When the Declaration of Independence was signed on July 4, 1776, proclaiming freedom and equality, it did not apply to enslaved African Americans. They continued to suffer under slavery despite the nation's declaration of liberty.

2. Historical Exclusion: African Americans were not considered full citizens and were excluded from the freedoms and rights celebrated on July 4th. This discrepancy between the ideals of freedom and the reality faced by enslaved and later, marginalized Black individuals, creates a disconnect with the holiday

Cultural and Social Impact

3. Juneteenth: For many African Americans, Juneteenth (June 19th) is a more significant celebration of freedom. It marks the day in 1865 when enslaved people in Texas were finally freed, over two years after the Emancipation Proclamation. Juneteenth represents a more meaningful celebration of liberation and is seen as a true reflection of African American freedom.

4. Recognition of Injustice: July 4th can serve as a reminder of the ongoing struggle for racial justice and equality. The celebration of independence can feel hollow when systemic racism and inequalities persist, making it difficult for some to fully embrace the holiday.

Modern Perspectives

5. Commemoration and Reflection: Some African Americans use July 4th as a day to reflect on the progress made, the struggles faced, and the continued work needed to achieve true equality. It can be a time to honor the legacy of those who fought for freedom and to address current social issues.

6. **Personal Famlily Tradition** For some African American families, July 4th might be celebrated in ways that honor both their heritage and the broader American context. This can include gatherings, educational activities, and community events that emphasize both pride in African American history and the complexities of the nation's history.

Why: Celebrating freedom and independence helps to reaffirm the values of liberty and self-determination. It inspires continued efforts towards achieving one's goals and dreams.

The ambivalence towards July 4th among African Americans reflects a nuanced understanding of American history and the ongoing pursuit of justice and equality. While the holiday is a significant American tradition, its celebration can be complicated by historical and social factors that influence how it is observed within the African American community. Our goal is always to educate and unify our communities in order to ensure Domestic Tranquility.

July Historical Reflection:

On July 2, 1964, the Civil Rights Act was signed into law, prohibiting discrimination based on race, color, religion, sex, or national origin.

Quote/Scripture: "It is for freedom that Christ has set us free. Stand firm, then, and do not let yourselves be burdened again by a yoke of slavery." (Galatians 5:1)

Prayer: Lord, as the United States celebrate Independence Day, we reflect on the true meaning of freedom for African Americans. As we celebrate the passage of the Civil Rights Act, we give thanks for the progress made towards equality. Let this month be a time of empowerment and action. Fill us with Your spirit of power, love, and self discipline. Guide us in our efforts to continue the work of justice and to make a positive impact in our communities. **Amen**

August: Wisdom and Learning Purpose:

August often signifies the end of summer and the beginning of new learning opportunities. Prayers in this month focus on seeking wisdom, guidance, and knowledge.

Why: As one prepares for new endeavors or educational pursuits, praying for wisdom and knowledge helps to prepare the mind and spirit for growth and learning.

August Historical Reflection:

In August 1963, the March on Washington for Jobs and Freedom took place, where Dr. King delivered his famous "I Have a Dream" speech.

Quote/Scripture: "For I can do everything through Christ, who gives me strength." (Philippians 4:13)

DIVINE RETRIBUTON

Prayer: Heavenly Father, as we enjoy the warmth of summer, let August be a time of rest and reflection. We remember the powerful message of Dr. Martin Luther King Jr. and the March on Washington. Let this month be a time of unity and action. Inspire us to work together towards love, justice, and equality. May we honor the dreams of those who came before us by striving for a better future. Fill us with Your peace and prepare us for the seasons ahead. **Amen.**

September: Preparation and Planning Purpose:

September is a time for preparation and planning as the year progresses towards its final months. Prayers focus on setting goals, planning for the future, and seeking divine guidance.

Why: Planning and preparation are crucial for achieving success. Seeking divine guidance ensures that plans align with God's purpose and are guided by spiritual insight.

September Historical Reflection:

In September 1957, the **Little Rock Nine integrated Central High School** in Arkansas, a significant event in the Civil Rights Movement.

Quote/Scripture: "The fear of the Lord is the beginning of wisdom, and knowledge of the Holy One is understanding." (Proverbs 9:10)

Prayer: Lord, as the school year begins, bless our students, teachers, and families. Let September be a month of learning, growth, and new opportunities. As we remember the courage of the Little Rock Nine, we pray for strength and determination in the face of adversity. Let this month be a time of bravery and progress. Guide us in your wisdom and our efforts to overcome challenges and to work towards equality and justice.

October: Reflection and Gratitude Purpose:

October is a time for reflection on the year's journey and expressing gratitude. Prayers focus on acknowledging progress, giving thanks, and preparing for the closing months of the year.

Why: Reflecting on the year's journey and expressing gratitude enhances spiritual growth and prepares the heart for a successful year-end.

October Historical Reflection:

In October 1966, the Black Panther Party was founded to challenge police brutality and systemic racism.

Quote/Scripture: "Let us not become weary in doing good, for at the proper time we will reap a harvest if we do not give up." (Galatians 6:9)

Prayer: As we reflect on the founding of the Black Panther Party, we pray for empowerment and justice in our communities. Help us to stand against oppression and to work towards a society where everyone is treated with fairness and respect. Guide us in our efforts to uplift and support one another. Father, during this harvest season, we thank You for Your provision. Let October be a time of gathering and gratitude, as we reflect on Your blessings. Amen.

November: Harvest and Abundance Purpose:

November represents a time of harvest and abundance. Prayers focus on recognizing and celebrating the fruits of one's labor and the blessings received throughout the year.

Why: Celebrating the harvest and acknowledging abundance reinforces a spirit of gratitude and encourages continued faith and trust in divine provision.

November Historical Reflection:

In November 2008, Barack Obama was elected as the first African American President of the United States.

Quote/Scripture: "Give thanks in all circumstances; for this is God's will for you in Christ Jesus." (1 Thessalonians 5:18)

Prayer As we celebrate the historic election of Barack Obama, we are reminded of the progress made and the potential within each of us. Fill us with the strength and courage to pursue our dreams and to create positive change in our world. May we be inspired by this milestone to continue striving for equality and justice for all. Gracious God, as we approach Thanksgiving, help us to cultivate a heart of gratitude. Let November be a month of reflection and appreciation for all You have done. **Amen.**

December: Reflection and Preparation for the New Year Purpose:

December is a time for reflecting on the year past and preparing for the new year. Prayers focus on closing out the year with gratitude and setting spiritual intentions for the coming year.

Why: Closing the year with reflection and preparation helps to transition smoothly into the new year with a sense of closure and renewed purpose.

December Historical Reflection:

In December 1955, Rosa Parks' refusal to give up her bus seat sparked the Montgomery Bus Boycott, a key event in the Civil Rights Movement.

Quote/Scripture: "And the peace of God, which transcends all understanding, will guard your hearts and your minds in Christ Jesus." (Philippians 4:7)

Prayer: Lord, as we prepare for Christmas, let December be a time of reflection and renewal. Fill our hearts with peace and joy, and remind us of the true meaning of this season. **Amen.**

PRAYER FOR BLACK TEACHERS

Heavenly Father, We come before You today with hearts full of gratitude and hope as we lift up our Black teachers who are returning to school. We thank You for their dedication, passion, and commitment to educating and nurturing the next generation. As they prepare to embark on a new school year, we ask for Your divine protection, guidance, and strength to be with them every step of the way.

Lord, we pray for wisdom and creativity for our Black teachers. Grant them the ability to inspire and engage their students, to foster a love for learning, and to encourage critical thinking and curiosity. May they be equipped with the tools and resources they need to create an inclusive and supportive classroom environment where every student feels valued and empowered.

We ask for Your protection over their health and well-being. Shield them from illness and harm, and provide them with the physical, emotional, and mental strength they need to navigate the challenges of teaching in these uncertain times. Surround them with a supportive community of colleagues, friends, and family who uplift and encourage them.

Lord, we also pray for the recognition and respect of our Black teachers. May their contributions be acknowledged and celebrated, and may they find joy and fulfillment in their work. Let them see the impact they are making in the lives of their students and feel appreciated for their hard work and dedication.

We pray for the students they teach, that they may be receptive and eager to learn. Help the students to respect and appreciate their teachers, and to understand the value of education. May the seeds of knowledge and wisdom that are planted in the classroom grow and flourish in the lives of the students, leading to bright futures and positive contributions to society.

Father, we ask that You empower our Black teachers with the courage and confidence to be strong role models and leaders in their communities. Let their light shine brightly, inspiring others to pursue their dreams and to strive for excellence. May they be a source of hope and inspiration to their students, colleagues, and the broader community.

We thank You, Lord, for the gift of education and for the incredible men and women who have answered the call to teach. Bless our Black teachers abundantly as they return to school, and may their efforts be fruitful and impactful. In Jesus' name, we pray. **Amen.**

Personal Retribution Prayer for Black Teachers

Our Father, I come before You today, acknowledging the struggles and triumphs of those who came before me and the path I now walk as a Black teacher. I thank You for the opportunity to educate and inspire the next generation. I seek Your guidance and strength as I strive to fulfill this calling with excellence and passion.

Physcial Restoration Lord, I pray for the physical strength and health needed to carry out my duties. Restore my energy and vitality daily. Protect me from any ailments or weariness that may hinder my ability to teach and nurture my students effectively.

Mental Restoration: Father, I ask for mental clarity and peace. Remove any anxiety, stress, or fear that may burden my mind. Fill me with Your wisdom and understanding, allowing me to approach each day with a sound mind and a positive outlook.

DIVINE RETRIBUTON

Creative Restoration: Creator God, I seek Your inspiration and creativity. Help me to develop engaging and innovative lessons that capture the imagination of my students. Restore any areas where my creativity has been stifled or undervalued, and let my ideas flourish for the benefit of my students.

Spiritual Restoration: Lord, restore my spirit and deepen my faith. Help me to remain rooted in Your Word and to draw strength from Your promises. Let my faith be a source of inspiration and encouragement to my students, guiding them towards hope and resilience.

Economic Restoration: Father, I pray for economic justice and provision. Restore any financial losses or disparities I have experienced. Open doors of opportunity for fair compensation and recognition of my contributions. Provide for my needs and bless me abundantly so I can be a blessing to others.

Social Restoration: Lord, restore my sense of community and belonging. Surround me with supportive colleagues, friends, and mentors who uplift and encourage me. Help me to build strong, positive relationships with my students and their families, fostering an environment of mutual respect and understanding.

Historical Restoration: Father, I acknowledge the historical injustices that have impacted Black educators and students. Restore the honor and dignity that has been stripped away. Let my work be a testament to the resilience and strength of my ancestors, and may I continue their legacy with pride and purpose.

Promises and Dreams Fulfillment: Heavenly Father, I call forth the promises, dreams, and visions of my ancestors into full manifestation. What they desired for themselves and did not receive, I claim it today on their behalf. Let their dreams live on through my actions and achievements. May their sacrifices be honored through the success and empowerment of my students.

Scripture Declaration: As it is written in Joel 2:25, "I will restore to you the years that the locust hath eaten, the cankerworm, and the caterpillar, and the palmerworm, my great army which I sent among you." I stand on this promise today, believing that You will restore all that has been lost. I declare that my efforts will be fruitful and impactful, and that I will experience the fullness of Your restoration in every area of my life. In Jesus' name, I pray. **Amen.**

NOTES   **DAY OF**

**DIVINE
RETRIBUTION**

HOLIDAY PRAYERS

Purpose: To reflect on the significance of the holiday, honor historical and cultural milestones, and seek divine guidance and blessings.

Why: Praying during significant holidays helps to connect with the meaning of the occasion, foster unity, and seek divine support and reflection on its significance. These prayers serve to ground the celebrations in spiritual significance, ensuring that the essence of each holiday is honored and celebrated with divine purpose.

New Year's Day: Purpose: To start the year with a fresh perspective, aligning intentions with divine purpose and seeking blessings for the year ahead.

Why: Praying on New Year's Day sets the tone for the entire year, inviting God's guidance and blessing for new beginnings.

New Year's Day/Eve Historical Reflection: On January 1, 1863, President Abraham Lincoln issued the Emancipation Proclamation, declaring freedom for enslaved people in Confederate states.

Quote/Scripture: "Therefore, if anyone is in Christ, the new creation has come: The old has gone, the new is here!" (2 Corinthians 5:17)

Prayer: Heavenly Father, As we step into a new year, we remember the significance of the Emancipation Proclamation and the promise of freedom it heralded. Let this New Year be a time of renewal and hope for us all. May we leave behind the burdens of the past and embrace the opportunities ahead with faith and courage. Guide us in Your wisdom, and help us to walk in the path of righteousness and justice. **Amen.**

Thanksgiving Historical Reflection

On November 1983, President Ronald Reagan signed a bill establishing Martin Luther King Jr. Day, honoring the legacy of the civil rights leader.

Quote/Scripture: "Give thanks to the Lord, for he is good; his love endures forever." (1 Chronicles 16:34)

Thanksgiving: Purpose: To give thanks for the blessings of the past year, acknowledge God's provision, and express gratitude for family, friends, and community.

: Thanksgiving prayers cultivate a heart of gratitude and recognition of God's blessings, reinforcing positive spiritual practices and relationships.

Thanksgiving Prayer

Gracious God, On this day of Thanksgiving, we gather to give thanks for the blessings You have bestowed upon us. We remember our ancestors, whose perseverance and courage paved the way for our freedoms today. As we share in this meal, we ask for Your continued blessings upon our families and communities. May our gratitude extend beyond this day, inspiring us to live with a heart of thankfulness and a spirit of giving. Amen.

Christmas Historical Reflection:

In December 1963, the Civil Rights Act was being fiercely debated, a pivotal moment in the fight for equality. Historical Reflection: On December 25, 1964, Dr. Martin Luther King Jr. delivered his "Christmas Sermon on Peace," advocating for nonviolence and brotherhood.

Quote/Scripture: "For unto us a child is born, unto us a son is given; and the government shall be upon his shoulder: and his name shall be called Wonderful, Counsellor, The mighty God, The everlasting Father, The Prince of Peace." (Isaiah 9:6)

Why: Christmas is a time of spiritual reflection and joy. Praying during this holiday enhances the celebration of Christ's birth and deepens the connection to His teachings.

Christmas Purpose: To celebrate the birth of Jesus Christ, reflect on His teachings, and express gratitude for the gift of salvation and grace.

Prayer: Dear Lord, As we celebrate the birth of Jesus Christ, we are reminded of the hope and light He brought into the world. Reflecting on the struggles for civil rights, we honor those who fought for justice and equality. Let the spirit of Christmas fill our hearts with love, compassion, and the courage to continue their legacy. May the Prince of Peace guide us in all our endeavors and bless our families with joy and unity. **Amen.**

Kwanzaa Prayer for Unity and Blessings

Kwanzaa is celebrated annually from **December 26 to January**. It is a week-long celebration that honors African heritage, culture, and values. Each day of Kwanzaa is dedicated to one of the seven principles known as the Nguzo Saba.

The seven principles of Kwanzaa, known as the Nguzo Saba, are central to the celebration and are meant to reinforce community values and culture.

1. **Umoja (Unity) Description**: Striving for and maintaining unity in the family, community, nation, and race.

Purpose: To promote unity and togetherness within the family and the broader community.

2. **Kujichagulia (SelfDetermination) Description**: Defining, naming, creating, and speaking for oneself.

Purpose: To encourage individuals to have control over their own destiny and selfidentity.

3. **Ujima (Collective Work and Responsibility) Description**: Building and maintaining our community together and making our brothers' and sisters' problems our problems and solving them together.

Purpose: To foster a sense of shared responsibility and collective problemsolving.

4. **Ujamaa (Cooperative Economics) Description**: Building and maintaining our own

stores, shops, and other businesses and profiting from them together.

Purpose: To support and uplift community businesses and economic selfsufficiency.

5. **Nia (Purpose) Description**: To make our collective vocation the building and developing of our community in order to restore our people to their traditional greatness.

Purpose: To set and pursue a common purpose that benefits the community.

6. **Kuumba (Creativity) Description:** Doing always as much as we can, in the way we can, in order to leave our community more beautiful and beneficial than we inherited it. Purpose: To encourage creativity and improvement in the community.

7. **Imani (Faith) Description**: Believing with all our heart in our people, our parents, our teachers, our leaders, and the righteousness and victory of our struggle.

Purpose: To instill and reinforce faith in oneself and the community.

Reference: Karenga, Maulana. *Kwanzaa: A Celebration of Family, Community, and Culture*. University of Sankore Press.

√These principles provide a framework for celebrating Kwanzaa and reinforcing cultural values within the African American community.

Easter is a major Christian holiday celebrating the resurrection of Jesus Christ from the dead, a central event in Christian faith.

DIVINE RETRIBUTON

It is considered the most important and oldest festival of the Christian Church.

Significance of Easter

1. **Resurrection of Jesus:** Description: Easter commemorates the resurrection of Jesus Christ on the third day after His crucifixion, as described in the New Testament of the Bible. Purpose: To celebrate the victory of life over death and the promise of eternal life for believers.

2. **Biblical Foundation:** Scriptures: Key scriptures include Matthew 28:56, Mark 16:6, Luke 24:67, and John 20:118, which narrate the discovery of the empty tomb and the resurrection of Jesus.

3. **Symbolism:** Symbols: Common symbols of Easter include the empty tomb, the cross, lilies, and the Easter egg, which symbolizes new life and rebirth.

4. **Celebration:** Observances: Traditions include attending church services, participating in Easter egg hunts, and sharing festive meals with family and friends. Suggested Prayer for Easter Easter

Easter Prayer

Heavenly Father, On this blessed Easter Sunday, we come before You with hearts full of gratitude and joy for the incredible gift of Your Son, Jesus Christ. We celebrate the resurrection of Jesus, the cornerstone of our faith, and the promise of eternal life that His victory over death brings to us.

Lord, we thank You for the sacrifice of Jesus and for the power of His resurrection, which gives us hope, redemption, and renewal. As we reflect on the empty tomb and the assurance of life everlasting, may we be reminded of Your boundless love and grace.

Help us to live each day in the light of the resurrection, embracing the new beginnings and opportunities that You provide. Grant us the strength to overcome our trials, the courage to follow

Your path, and the joy of sharing the message of Your salvation with others. As we celebrate with family and friends, let our hearts be filled with the peace and joy that comes from knowing Christ's resurrection.

May the power of this holy day inspire us to live out our faith with renewed vigor and to spread Your love and grace to all whom we meet. In the name of Jesus, who conquered death and gave us the gift of eternal life, we pray. **Amen.**

PRAYERS FOR THE 4 SEASONS

WINTER PRAYER

Historical Reflection: In the winter of 1963-64, the Mississippi Freedom Winter saw civil rights activists working tirelessly to register African American voters.

In the winter of 1955-1956, the Montgomery Bus Boycott took place, led by Rosa Parks and Dr. Martin Luther King Jr. This pivotal event in the Civil Rights Movement exemplified the power of collective action and resilience.

Prayer:

Heavenly Father, As we enter the season of winter, we reflect on the strength and unity demonstrated during the Montgomery Bus Boycott. As we embrace the season, we reflect on the progress made towards ending segregation. Let this season of stillness and reflection renew our commitment to justice and equality.

Purify our hearts and minds, and guide us in our efforts to bring about positive change. We ask for Your guidance and support in our own struggles for justice and equality. Help us to stand firm in our convictions and work together to create a better world. May the cold of winter remind us of the warmth of community and the power of perseverance.

As we embrace the stillness of winter, we remember the perseverance and courage of those who fought for our right to vote. Just as the snow blankets the earth, cover us with Your peace and grace. Let this season be one of reflection and renewal, as we seek to deepen our relationship with You and strengthen our commitment to justice and equality.**Amen**

Inspirational Quote/Scripture: "But those who hope in the Lord will renew their strength. They will soar on wings like eagles; they will run and not grow weary, they will walk and not be faint." (Isaiah 40:31)

Spring Prayer

Historical Reflection: In the spring of 1965, the Selma to Montgomery marches galvanized the nation and led to the passage of the Voting Rights Act.

Quote/Scripture: "Behold, I will do a new thing; now it shall spring forth; shall ye not know it? I will even make a way in the wilderness and rivers in the desert." (Isaiah 43:19)

Prayer: Lord, As the earth awakens and new life springs forth, we remember the bravery of those who marched for our freedom and rights. Let this season of spring be a time of growth and renewal in our lives. May we blossom in our faith and our endeavors, and may Your spirit guide us in all we do. **Amen.**

Summer Prayer

Historical Reflection: In the summer of 1964, Freedom Summer aimed to increase voter registration in Mississippi, marked by both great progress and tremendous sacrifice.

Quote/Scripture: "So if the Son sets you free, you will be free indeed." (John 8:36)

Prayer: Dear Lord, As we bask in the warmth of summer, we honor the sacrifices made for our freedoms. Let this season be one of abundance and joy, as we gather with loved ones and celebrate the progress we have made. Fill our hearts with gratitude and inspire us to continue the work of those who came before us. **Amen.**

Fall Prayer

Historical Reflection

In the fall of 1961, the Albany Movement was a significant chapter in the Civil Rights Movement, focusing on the desegregation of an entire community.

Quote/Scripture: "The Lord is my light and my salvation; whom shall I fear? The Lord is the strength of my life; of whom shall I be afraid?" (Psalm 27:1)

Prayer: Gracious God, As we transition into the fall, we reflect on the movements that brought about change and justice. Let this season be one of harvest, where we reap the fruits of our labor and the seeds planted by our ancestors. May we find strength in Your light and courage in Your love as we continue their legacy. **Amen.**

NOTES **DAY OF**

**DIVINE
RETRIBUTION**

PRAYER TIME MANAGEMENT

Plan and manage your weekly prayers like it was your job

1 Monday

2 Tuesday

3 Wednesday

4 Thursday

5 Friday

6 Saturday

7 Sunday

NOTES   **DAY OF**

DIVINE RETRIBUTION

NOTES   DAY OF

DIVINE
RETRIBUTION

To do list

Start to plan your goals based on the prayers you learned

In 6 months from now I want to achieve...

- [ ] _____
- [ ] _____
- [ ] _____
- [ ] _____
- [ ] _____

Step By Step To Activate

In 12 months from now I want to achieve... **BE BOLD-BE COURAGEOUS**

- _____

- _____

- _____

- _____

- _____

ACKNOWLEDGEMENTS

First and foremost, I extend my deepest gratitude to the Almighty God, whose guidance and inspiration have been the foundation of this work. This book is a testament to His promises of restoration and retribution.

Research and Inspiration

I would like to acknowledge the invaluable contributions of historians, scholars, and researchers whose work provided the historical and cultural context for this book. Their dedication to uncovering and documenting the stories of African American inventors, creators, and pioneers has enriched this manuscript.

Special Thanks To:

Historians and Scholars: For their extensive research and writings on African American history and contributions. - Biographers and Authors: Whose works on notable figures have been a source of inspiration and information. - Religious Leaders and Theologians: For their insights into scriptural promises and prayers that have guided the spiritual elements of this book.

Credits Historical Facts and Figures:

The stories and achievements of African American inventors, artists, and pioneers mentioned in this book have been sourced from a variety of scholarly articles, biographies, and historical texts. Some notable sources include:

The African American Inventor's Museum - "African American History and Culture by African American History and Culture" by Dr. John Hope Franklin and Lynn M. Dumenil. This book provides a comprehensive overview of African American history and culture, detailing contributions and injustice

Black Inventors and Their Inventions by Keith C. Holmes. This book offers an in- depth look at African American inventors and their contributions, highlighting the struggles and achievements of black inventors throughout history.

Scriptural References:

Scriptures and biblical promises are quoted from various translations of the Bible. For accuracy and context, the following translations have been used: - New International Version (NIV) - King James Version (KJV) Quotes and Inspiration: Inspirational quotes included in this book are sourced from a variety of public and historical figures whose words have motivated and uplifted. For exact quotations and contexts, please refer to the bibliographic references included.

Special Recognition

Family and Friends: To my family and friends who provided unwavering support and encouragement throughout this journey—your belief in this project has been a source of strength. Contributors and

Collaborators: A heartfelt thank you to those who provided feedback, suggestions, and edits that enhanced the quality and impact of this book.

References

A comprehensive list of references used in the creation of this book, including books, articles, and online resources, is provided in the bibliography section. These sources have been instrumental in shaping the content and ensuring its accuracy.

Legal Disclaimer

This book contains prayers and reflections intended for spiritual enrichment and historical education. All quotes and scriptures are used with respect and in accordance with copyright laws.

Credits

National Museum of African American History and Culture. "African American Inventors." Smithsonian Institution, www.nmaahc.si.edu/explore/stories/african- american-inventors. Accessed 15 Aug. 2024.

Library of Congress. "Notable African American Figures." Library of Congress, www.loc.gov/collections/notable-african-american-figures. Accessed 20 Aug. 2024.

Government Documents U.S. Patent Office. Records of African American Inventors. Government Printing Office, 2018.

HALL OF FAME DEDICATION PAGE

This page is dedicated to the countless African Americans whose contributions have gone unrecognized and untold. These names represent the hundreds, if not thousands, of brilliant minds and talented souls whose stories remain hidden in the shadows of history. Their legacy, like the lost books of the Bible, holds untold wisdom and greatness that one day, God will reveal in full. This testament stands in honor of their enduring impact and the rich heritage they left behind. May their spirits inspire us to continue uncovering and celebrating the profound contributions of all those who came before us.

To all the ancestors and their immeasurable contributions. To the brilliant African Americans, both living and deceased.

To every inventor, creator, author, and visionary who was never given credit.

To all the mothers who never held their children, and all the fathers who never got to raise them.

To the countless soldiers who paved theway in war and those whose minds were used to better the country but were never honored.

This book is a tribute to your resilience, creativity, and unrecognized excellence.

We honor you, remember you, and continue your legacy.

TRIBUTE UNRECOGNIZED AFRICAN AMERICAN INNOVATORS

This is a short list from the many heroes and sheroes who went without just dues. These individuals represent the countless African Americans whose contributions have gone unrecognized and untold. Their stories, like the lost books of the Bible, hold untold wisdom and greatness that one day, God will reveal in full. This testament stands in honor of their enduring impact and the rich heritage they left behind. May their spirits inspire us to continue uncovering and celebrating the profound contributions of all those who came before us.

In Memory Of

1. **Granville T. Woods (1856-1910)** Contribution: Known as the "Black Edison," Granville T. Woods was an inventor who held more than 60 patents. His inventions included the multiplex telegraph, which allowed multiple messages to be sent over a single wire, and significant improvements to railroad and electrical systems. Legacy: Despite his prolific output, Woods often had to fight for recognition and ownership of his inventions, sometimes facing legal battles with other inventors like Thomas Edison.

2. **Lewis Howard Latimer (1848-1928)** Contribution: Latimer was a key figure in the development of the electric light bulb, working alongside Alexander Graham Bell and Thomas Edison. He improved the filament in light bulbs, making them more durable and longerlasting. Legacy: While Edison is widely celebrated, Latimer's contributions are less wellknown, despite his crucial role in making electric lighting practical and widespread.

3. Henrietta Lacks (1920-1951) Contribution: Lacks's cells, taken without her knowledge or consent, became the first immortal human cell line, known as HeLa cells. These cells have been used in countless medical breakthroughs, including the development of the polio vaccine, cancer treatments, and AIDS research. Legacy: Lacks never received recognition or compensation during her lifetime, and her story highlights significant ethical issues in medical research.

4. Dr. Charles Drew (1904-1950) Contribution: Dr. Drew was a pioneer in blood banking and transfusion. He developed improved techniques for blood storage and established large scale blood banks during World War II, which saved countless lives. Legacy: Despite his groundbreaking work, Drew faced racial discrimination and was often denied opportunities that were readily available to his white counterparts.

5. Marie Van Brittan Brown (1922-1999) Contribution: Brown invented the first home security system in 1966, which included closed circuit television surveillance. Her invention laid the groundwork for modern security systems. Legacy: Although Brown's invention was patented, she did not receive the widespread recognition she deserved during her lifetime.

6. Garrett Morgan (1877-1963) Contribution: Morgan invented the traffic signal and the gas mask. His safety hood was used by firefighters, and his traffic signal design significantly improved road safety. Legacy: While his inventions had a significant impact, Morgan's contributions were often overshadowed by the racial prejudices of his time.

7. Sarah Boone (1832-1904) Contribution: Boone improved the ironing board, making it more effective for ironing garments, particularly women's clothing. Her design is the basis for modern ironing boards. Legacy: Boone was one of the first African American women to receive a patent, but her contributions remain largely unrecognized in the broader narrative of American innovation.

8. Dr. Patricia Bath (1942-2019) Contribution: Dr. Bath was the first African American woman to receive a medical patent. She invented the Laserphaco Probe, a device that improved the treatment of cataracts. Legacy: Despite her significant contributions to ophthalmology, Dr. Bath's achievements are not as widely celebrated as they should be.

9. **Madam C.J. Walker** (1867-1919) Contribution The first female self made millionaire in America, she created a line of hair care products for Black women but faced significant racial and gender discrimination.

10. Elijah McCoy's (1843-1929) oil drip cup invention for trains was so successful that people began asking for "the real McCoy," though he faced barriers in patenting and promoting his inventions.

11. Dr. Patricia Bath (1942 - 2019) Invented the Laserphaco Probe for cataract treatment but struggled for recognition in the predominantly white field of ophthalmology.

12. Alice H. Parker (1895-1920?) Developed an early concept for central heating using natural gas, but her work was largely overlooked in history.

13 **Edmonia Lewis** (1844-1907) A pioneering sculptor of mixed African American and Native American heritage, her work gained acclaim but was often marginalized in the art world

14. Augusta Savage (1892 - 1962) A renowned sculptor and educator during the Harlem Renaissance, she created works that celebrated Black culture but struggled for recognition and support.

15. **Henry Ossawa Tanner** (1859-1937): An influential painter who faced racial discrimination in the U.S. and moved to France, where he found greater acceptance

16. **Jean-Michel Basquiat** (1960-1988): A groundbreaking artist whose works often addressed racial and social issues, but he battled exploitation and marginalization during his career.

17. **Billie Holiday** (1915-1959): A legendary jazz and blues singer known for her emotive voice and powerful songs like "Strange Fruit," but she faced systemic racism and personal struggles

18. **Robert Johnson** (1911-1938): A pioneering blues guitarist whose recordings influenced countless musicians, yet he received little recognition or financial reward in his lifetime.

19. **Ma Rainey** (1886-1939): Known as the "Mother of the Blues," she was a major influence on blues music but received far less recognition than her white counterparts.

20. **Nina Simone** (1933-2003): An iconic singer and civil rights activist whose music addressed social issues, but she faced significant obstacles in her career due to racism.

21. **Josephine Baker** (1906-1975): A trailblazing performer and activist who found fame in France but faced discrimination in the United States.

22. **Ethel Waters** (1896-1977): A groundbreaking singer and actress who broke racial barriers in entertainment but often faced typecasting and limited opportunities. Writers and Intellectuals

23. **Zora Neale Hurston** (1891-1960): A prominent writer and anthropologist during the Harlem Renaissance, her work was often overlooked during her lifetime.

24. **Langston Hughes** (1902-1967): A central figure in the Harlem Renaissance, his poetry and writing were influential but he faced persistent racism and financial struggles.

25. **Phillis Wheatley** (1753-1784): The first published African American female poet, her work was often dismissed or marginalized by contemporary critics.

26. **James Baldwin** (1924-1987): A powerful voice in literature and civil rights, his work confronted racial and social issues, but he faced significant opposition and marginalization.

Actors and Dancers

27. **Paul Robeson** (1898-1976): An acclaimed actor, singer, and activist, he faced severe backlash and blacklisting due to his outspoken views on civil rights.

28. **Dorothy Dandridge** (1922-1965): The first African American actress nominated for an Academy Award for Best Actress, she faced significant barriers in Hollywood.

29. **Katherine Dunham** (1909-2006): A pioneering dancer and choreographer who incorporated African and Caribbean styles into modern dance but struggled for recognition and funding.

30. **Hattie McDaniel** (1893-1952): The first African American to win an Academy Award, she faced discrimination and typecasting throughout her career.

31 . **Alvin Ailey** (1931-1989): A visionary choreographer who founded the Alvin Ailey American Dance Theater, which promoted African American cultural expression in dance, yet he faced funding and recognition challenges.

These entries provide a deeper understanding of the contributions and struggles of these influential African Americans, and they emphasize the depth of the injustice faced by Black inventors, artists, and performers throughout history.

PRAYERS AND REFLECTION FOR THREE INNOVATORS

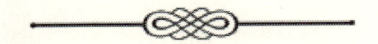

Father, We lift up the names and contributions of those African Americans whose brilliance and innovations have shaped our world. We honor their legacies and seek justice for their stolen ideas and unrecognized work.

May their stories inspire us to strive for truth, equity, and recognition for all who contribute to the betterment of humanity. Amen. Reflection on Resilience and Innovation As we reflect on the lives of these innovators, we are reminded of their resilience and determination in the face of adversity.

Their stories teach us the importance of perseverance, the power of creativity, and the impact of their contributions. Let us honor their legacies by continuing to fight for justice and equality in all fields of endeavors.

Quote/Scripture:

"Do not conform to the pattern of this world, but be transformed by the renewing of your mind." (Romans 12:2) This scripture encourages us to continue innovating and pushing boundaries, just as these pioneers did, despite the challenges they faced.

NOTES　　　　　　　　　　　　　　　　　　　DAY OF

**DIVINE
RETRIBUTION**

There is no end to this journey or these prayers... You will return here again and again, and each day will be even more powerful than the day before. All I ask of you is this: Take someone on this journey with you. Share it with every African American you know.

How To Stay In touch with drfaye

DIVINE RETRIBUTON

Contact:coach@drfaye.com Office 1 1-501-360-9758 www.kingdomwomenarerising.com and christianwomenimpact.com